Marching Orders from
Rabbi Adin Even-Israel Steinsaltz

Marching Orders from Rabbi Adin Even-Israel Steinsaltz

KABBALAH

Compiled by Arthur Kurzweil

AN ARTHUR KURZWEIL BOOK
New York/Jerusalem

© 2019 Arthur Kurzweil
All rights reserved

No part of this book may be used or reproduced in any manner whatsoever without the prior express written permission of the author, except in the case of brief quotations embodied in critical articles and reviews. Please do not participate in or encourage piracy of copyrighted material in violation of the author's rights.

Profits from the sale of this book
will go to the Aleph Society.
The Aleph Society exists to support the work of Rabbi Adin Even-Israel Steinsaltz around the globe, and his mission to make the Talmud and other sources of Jewish knowledge accessible to all Jews.

Books by Rabbi Adin Even-Israel Steinsaltz are available from www.korenpub.com.

Cover and interior design by Judith M. Tulli.

*Marching Orders from
Rabbi Adin Even-Israel Steinsaltz: Kabbalah*
This is the second in a series.

ISBN: 978-1-7321749-2-4

To my mind, Kabbalah is the theology
of the Jewish people.

— Rabbi Adin Even-Israel Steinsaltz

Compiler's Introduction

This small book, *Kabbalah*, is the second in a series of what I have called "Marching Orders."

In an essay about the Lubavitcher Rebbe, Rabbi Steinsaltz writes, "The Rebbe did not leave a legacy ... The Rebbe left *marching orders*. This is an entirely different concept. The Rebbe did not just leave a collection of books, videos, and speeches. He left a task to be completed."

Rabbi Steinsaltz has thousands of students throughout the world, but there is no uniform to wear, no organization to join, no world headquarters, no franchises, and no rules to follow. "Basically I am a teacher," says the Rabbi.

Unlike so many so-called spiritual leaders, Rabbi Adin Even-Israel Steinsaltz has never appeared to be interested in creating followers.

Most say, "Come." Rabbi Steinsaltz says, "Go."

Most say, "Mimic me." Rabbi Steinsaltz says, "Be yourself."

Most say, "Follow me." Rabbi Steinsaltz says, "Challenge me."

Most say, "Obey." Rabbi Steinsaltz says, "Learn."

Yet scattered throughout the Rabbi's books and lectures, and embedded within his commentaries, Rabbi Steinsaltz offers advice and perspectives on many subjects. The Rabbi's approach — though difficult, perhaps impossible, to summarize — is unique and compelling.

I have chosen and gathered some of the Rabbi's teachings and presented them in the following pages. They have been selected from throughout the Rabbi's published and unpublished works as a result of my search to develop a kind of "Steinsaltzian" set of marching orders for current and future students.

— Arthur Kurzweil

Kabbalah

Kabbalah's mystifying formulas become nothing more than intoxicating mantras to those who mindlessly repeat them. This is like trying to cure an illness by chanting the chemical formula of the remedy. This is not to say that Kabbalah should not be studied and learned. In fact, it is incumbent upon Jewish scholars to understand the whole map of Torah from beginning to end, the Hidden Law no less than the Revealed Law. Throughout history, there have been those who, very quietly, achieved extensive knowledge of the Hidden Law.

An essay, "Kabbalah for Today?"

The word *spiritual* has unfortunately acquired mystical and supernatural connotations, and is used too frequently by all kinds of unreliable people, from bleary-eyed old ladies speaking about spirituality to quacks selling spiritual medicines and spiritual workshops that will make us wise, beautiful, successful, and thin. Since such "spirituality" seems to range from wishy-washy to clinically crazy, it is not at all astonishing that some people keep a safe distance.

The spiritual world we live in is very close and real. It is not the realm of ghosts and disembodied beings, where powers and vibrations (whatever they are) roam. The spiritual world is, first and foremost, all the things we relate to through our minds. This includes our thoughts and emotions, love, hate, and envy, the ability to read, to enjoy music, or to solve equations, to know that we exist, and to relate to others. All these are intangible — they cannot be touched or weighed. However, they are commonplace, direct experiences, and they are as real as anything can be. All these together make up our second world, the spiritual one.

"Spirit and Matter," in *Simple Words: Thinking About What Really Matters in Life*

Kabbalah literally means "receiving." In Israel today, the receipt you get when making a purchase is called a *kabbalah*. The Bible, or Written Law, is given by God and is available to anyone who can read it. The Oral Law — which includes the Kabbalah — is received, passed directly from teacher to pupil. Most of Torah is considered *Torah haniglet* — revealed Torah, to be studied by all Jews. Kabbalah, however, was designated *chochmah nisteret* — hidden wisdom. In truth, Kabbalah was never literally hidden, but was not widely, or even publicly, studied. The reason for restricting the study of Kabbalah relates to its subject matter.

An essay, "Kabbalah for Today?"

To my mind, Kabbalah is the theology of the Jewish people.

Preface to *The Thirteen Petalled Rose: A Discourse on the Essence of Jewish Existence and Belief*

Breaking of the vessels (*shvirat ha-kelim*) is a basic kabbalistic concept describing what happened prior to the reality in which we live. All of reality is composed of lights and vessels; and when the lights are too numerous for the vessels, the latter break because they cannot contain the light. This breaking of the vessels creates an intermingled reality that lacks clear direction and meaning, for the vessels become entities discrete from the light; instead of revealing the light, they conceal it. To illustrate this, when letters compose a word, they become a vessel containing meaning (or light), but when the word is "broken" and the letters separated, they no longer express that light.

Glossary to *Opening the Tanya: Discovering the Moral and Mystical Teachings of a Classic Work of Kabbalah*

Kabbalah is not a separate area of Torah knowledge but rather the hidden, spiritual dimension of the revealed aspects of the Torah. Whereas the revealed aspects of the Torah, such as Halakhah, speak primarily about visible, physical things, Kabbalah speaks directly about spiritual entities. It speaks of the system of "Worlds" and *sefirot* through which God creates, sustains, and directs the universe; and it discusses the interaction between those spiritual entities and the performance of *mitzvot* in the physical world. Hence, Kabbalah has been called the soul of the Torah.

Glossary to *Opening the Tanya: Discovering the Moral and Mystical Teachings of a Classic Work of Kabbalah*

If there is a normative Jewish theology, it is the integration of the two (never really separate) approaches — the Kabbalah of the Ari and the Shulhan Arukh of Rabbi Joseph Caro. This was possible because, unlike most mystical schools in the world, which somehow stressed their freedom from the constraints of formal religion (even when they continued to remain within it), Kabbalah mysticism did the opposite. It always stressed the vital significance of the smallest details of the law and the ritual. The kabbalists even added weight and meaning to the formal practices in a thousand ways. And when it came to such issues of theoretical theology as the Thirteen Articles of Faith, they simply put different emphasis on the same words. To be sure, they had their disagreements with some of Maimonides' ideas; nevertheless, they did not let disagreement develop into friction and antagonism. Everything in the tradition was somehow incorporated into the kabbalistic framework with a certain broad spiritual comprehensiveness. What is astonishing, at least to the rational thinking of the Western world, is that there were no great contradictions, that the two modes of religiosity worked together as well as they did.

"Mysticism in the Jewish Tradition," in *On Being Free*

There was never a separation of any real consequence between the daily obligations and open practice of Judaism and the esoteric or mystical aspects of the tradition. They have always been connected. They are simply different aspects of the same thing. In the Middle Ages many scholars leaned almost entirely on the writings of Maimonides and pointed to his Thirteen Articles of Faith as the supreme theological authority. But even in those times there was more than one approach to theology. For example, we also have the more mystical approach of Rabbi Moshe ben Nachman (the Ramban). But since there was no central authority to define a consensus of opinion, the differences — which, as intimated, were never as polarized as modern thinkers believe — were allowed to flourish. It is only since the sixteenth century that there has been a consensus accepted by almost every Jew. If there is a normative Jewish theology, it is the integration of the two (never really separate) approaches — the Kabbalah of the Ari and the Shulhan Arukh of Rabbi Joseph Caro.

"Mysticism in the Jewish Tradition," in *On Being Free*

The evil in the world is derived from a distortion of certain forces, and they can, in turn, have a bad effect on the rest of creation. The Torah, or Jewish Scriptures, is, on the whole, a revelation of the right way to behave so that the Divine plenty will flow into the reality of the world. The carrying out of the commandments (*mitzvot*) of the Torah acts in a concrete way to make the *sefirot* combine properly to cause this plenty to flow, while the transgression of the commandments is an act of absolute evil that adds strength to the forces of wickedness and pollution in the world. The esoteric teaching, the Kabbalah, is the inner part of the Torah that explains the metaphysical significance of every single movement and thought, and ultimately of the whole essence of the world. The man who attains genuine knowledge of the wisdom of the Kabbalah can, in certain respects, use the keys provided by this wisdom to reach a deeper and more complete closeness to God, and is able to change and "repair" the world in which he lives.

"The Ari," in *The Strife of the Sprit*

Ultimately, high theology and high philosophy can only answer the question, "What is God?" with the answer of a newborn baby, "God is the wholeness of everything." The mystical writings say things about God that every child knows. In the words of the Zohar, "God, You are the completeness of everything." The understanding of God as "the completeness of everything" is quite simple, and it is not an anthropomorphic picture of God. It is not an image that people can visualize. This understanding is so close and integral that it is almost invisible.

On the other hand, it is a very abstract notion, and difficult to express in words. Children are usually too young to articulate their belief, and by the time they develop consciousness and language, they can see the world only as disjointed pieces. Perhaps earlier, the child understands the oneness, and if no one spoils that belief, he will have it, wherever and however he lives. The secret of belief is not to expect to see miracles ... but rather to preserve the innate notion we are born with. Instead of adding, we have to edit out so many extra, useless words and ideas. If we can come to the core, and carefully develop the very fundamental points of our minds, we may discover that God has always existed within us.

"God," in *Simple Words: Thinking About What Really Matters in Life*

The study of Jewish mysticism, the Kabbalah, presents a special problem. Though the Kabbalah is probably the only extant Jewish theological system, there are various attitudes to its study, which question not the relative value of studying Kabbalah, but the qualifications necessary to undertake it. It is very important to recognize that, unlike other mystical doctrines, the Kabbalah is not a discipline unto itself but is closely linked to mainstream religious practice. It is in a sense a commentary on both the written and oral Torah, and cannot be separated either in theory or practice from the full panoply of the *mitzvot*.

"Talmud Torah," in *Teshuvah: A Guide for the Newly Observant Jew*

Marching Orders

There is a story of Rabbi Shimshon of Ostropol, who is famous for his two books on Kabbalah. It is told that he decided one day to write a complete kabbalistic commentary on the Talmud, to explain the secret and hidden meanings of this enormous body of Jewish learning. He made good use of his knowledge of esoteric wisdom and completed the complex work after considerable labor. But being a very holy man, he subjected the book to the test of a dream, known as *she'eilat halom*, and the answer he got to his questions was that his work was too lengthy and elaborate. He made it shorter and again posed the question. The answer was the same: too long. Again he cut his work down, and again he was told that it was not sufficiently precise and clear. When he had made it as short and concise as he could, he discovered that what he had written was *Perush Rashi*, the accepted commentary on the Talmud.

"Mysticism in the Jewish Tradition," in *On Being Free*

The tradition of the Chain of Receiving (*Shalshelet Ha-Kabbalah*) is basically the tradition of Jewish leadership. It is a listing of a certain number of the more prominent persons who were bearers of the light of knowledge; it does not deny that there were others who also carried it. The point of the chain is that there was a continuity, an uninterrupted flow.

"After the Bright Light of Revelation," in *Parabola*

From the period following the expulsion from Spain (beginning with the sixteenth century CE), study of the Kabbalah became more widespread, making what had once been the heritage of a few small groups an inseparable part of general Torah study. The major center in the city of Safed — which served as a kind of spiritual center for the Jewish people in those days — was the home of some of the greatest halakhic scholars, who also engaged in kabbalistic study, as well as of many great kabbalists and poets.

Introduction to *A Guide to Jewish Prayer*

The relations between man and woman are part of the inner dynamics of the world. And perhaps, at least for the sake of the literary imagination of humanity, it's just as well that this is so. For besides the need for novels and stories, there is the need for separation — and not only of the sexes — in order for creative tension to be generated. In the Kabbalah it is known as the Secret of the Cleavage, Sod HaNisirah, which has its origin in the very first stages of Creation when the firmament was made, to separate the waters, forming the upper waters and the lower waters, with the eternal tension between them.

"The Great Awe of Pachad Yitzchak," in *In the Beginning: Discourses on Chasidic Thought*

Although a careful distinction was maintained throughout these centuries between the *nigleh* and the *nistar*, between the revealed and the hidden aspects of the religion, it was never a division within Judaism as conceived by its greatest authorities. The Shulhan Arukh, the great work that has become the fundamental halakhic text for all of Jewry, was written by Rabbi Joseph Caro, a sage whose authority rested not only on his very broad learning but also on his many-sidedness and mystic insight. He wrote other books of halakhic procedure and law, exegeses on Torah and the like, and in addition he wrote a treatise called Maggid Mesharim, which was certainly a kabbalistic work and showed him to be a man who had mystical experiences and visions. Those of his generation who heard about his revelations were inclined to say it was the voice of the Mishnah speaking from his mouth. To this day, the inspired orders of prayers we follow on the all-night *tikun* of Shavuot are those of Rabbi Joseph Caro. And one of his closest disciples wrote the famous Shabbat song "Lechah Dodi," now accepted in all circles of Jewish worship, which is obviously a kabbalistic poem. So we see that the greatest of the halakhic legal authorities was very much immersed in the mystical world of Kabbalah.

"Mysticism in the Jewish Tradition," in *On Being Free*

Precisely because of the prevalence of metaphorical statement, and the widespread use of figures of speech drawn from the human image, it becomes all the more necessary to emphasize that they are allegorical truths and not actual descriptions of reality. For there was a certain danger that the word pictures, or imagistic descriptions, of sacred symbols in the Bible — and even more so in the Kabbalah — could lead to a crude material apprehension of the Divine essence and of the higher reality. Hence the prohibition against all depiction of holiness through physical, plastic means. Accompanying it, and perhaps stemming from this extreme revulsion to plastic semblance of the Divine, Jewish tradition also maintains a certain suspicion of man's tendency to design, elaborate, and portray himself.

"The Human Image," in *The Thirteen Petalled Rose: A Discourse on the Essence of Jewish Existence and Belief*

A facet of *gevurah* is that of the feminine, as opposed to the masculine facet of *chesed*. Here one has to remember that in Kabbalah we cannot apply the same rigidity of thought as in biology. What is of value for our purpose is the fact that the relationship between male and female is one of the most rudimentary ones in an extremely complex system of relations, human and otherwise. It is human and beyond the human also in the way we divide the lines of the *sefirot* into masculine and feminine forces, as influencing factors and those receiving influence, as right and left.

"The Power to Accept," in *In the Beginning: Discourses on Chasidic Thought*

A little knowledge is a dangerous thing in any field. As far as Torah is concerned, since it is a live wire connecting us with God, anyone who gets involved without taking precautionary measures runs the risk of being electrocuted. It was in this sense that Kabbalah used to be considered a field that was not accessible to all. There was a need for special knowledge and sensitivity to be able to enter into the realm of the hidden. When studying the Talmud, it is all too apparent when one does not quite comprehend a passage, because the Talmud speaks about people, animals, the mundane affairs of men. A student can easily discern what he grasps and what he does not. But when studying Kabbalah — which speaks about *sefirot*, angels, Divine lights, and vessels — the ability to distinguish one's own lack of understanding is far more difficult, so that the subtle danger of misconception is a sad inevitability. All of this is not intended to divert attention from the fact that the Torah, including the manifest and the hidden, is all one. To be sure, it is said that it has seventy faces. Indeed, some sources say it has six hundred thousand faces, because that is the number of souls who received the Torah when it was revealed, and each one has, to this day, his own understanding of it, his own orientation and point of view.

"Mysticism in the Jewish Tradition," in *On Being Free*

The Kabbalah is hidden, not just by language, but by a very difficult style, by a myriad of almost incomprehensible formulas.

Preface to *The Thirteen Petalled Rose: A Discourse on the Essence of Jewish Existence and Belief*

The Kabbalah, the mystical doctrine of Judaism, is the "inner" teachings concerning the significance and secret meanings of the Torah, which goes hand in hand with the revealed Torah. The earliest rudiments of these mystical teachings seem to have been systematically taught at the centers of study for the disciples of the prophets, known as Sons of the Prophets (II Kings 2:3, and elsewhere). Such teachings were naturally available only to the choice few who wished, and were able, to comprehend them.

Introduction to *A Guide to Jewish Prayer*

In the late Middle Ages, books begin to appear on these subjects, originating from two different schools: Hassidei Ashkenaz (The Pious Ones of Franco-Germany) and Hakhmei Sepharad (The Sages of Spain). Even in those days, such study was limited to a few small, closed groups, albeit it is possible to trace the influence of mystic thought on the prayer liturgy. One indication of this influence is found in the various *piyutim* composed by these pious sages. But its influence was felt primarily in emendations and revisions of the prayer text. Various esoteric traditions relating to the number of words, or even the number of letters, in certain prayers and benedictions, as well as stylistic and linguistic details, were all directed by the mystic tradition and introduced into the fixed liturgical texts.

Introduction to *A Guide to Jewish Prayer*

The "work of prayer," in brief, consists of being in tune, paying progressively deeper attention to what one is saying until one's heart is in tune with one's words. This inner work precedes prayer itself. Like the foundation of a building, it is the basis of one's concentration — whether it is the mystical unifications of the Ari or "praying like this little child." There is a world of difference between focused attention based on kabbalistic secrets, in which the words of prayer are understood on a profound plane, and simple prayer, which focuses on the literal meaning of the words. But they both possess the same necessary foundation: attention to what one is saying. If a person recites a prayer that is not his — if he is merely speaking someone else's words — that is not truly prayer. A person should mean truly what he says; on whatever level he speaks, it should be the reality in which he lives and prays. The main point of prayer is that "I am praying." When I am saying my own prayer, then it is on a very high level.

"Prayer," in *The Thirteen Petalled Rose: A Discourse on the Essence of Jewish Existence and Belief*

Regarding the mystery of birth, let us say that the body of the child is formed from the cells of the father and mother. The soul of the child, however, is formed by neither, but rather is created by a "copulation" of the *sefirot*. When the *sefirot* mix with one another, they give birth to souls and these souls are combinations of *sefirot* in an infinite variety of relations. Every time and in every place where there is a new combination (usually the combinations are old, fairly fixed), a new soul is born.

"The Power to Accept," in *In the Beginning: Discourses on Chasidic Thought*

We know that since Second Temple times the study of the hidden mysteries of the Torah has been considered the highest level of Torah teaching, and was conducted in the framework of the story of creation (Ma'aseh Bereshit, Genesis I) and the story of the Divine Chariot (Ma'aseh Merkavah, Ezekiel I). As the contents of these teachings were kept secret, we know only how they influenced the formulation of prayer, both in the Temple and outside it, from certain hints. It is quite clear, however, that the sages who composed the prayers encoded within them concepts and key words derived from the realm of hidden, mystic thought.

Introduction to *A Guide to Jewish Prayer*

All Torah study is based on an acceptance of tradition and on the principle that, because the Torah is a Divine gift, a person must make himself into a proper vessel in order to receive it. In the study of Kabbalah, however, these approaches are even more important. Because Kabbalah is the inner spiritual dimension of the Torah, the individual must study it in a way that engages his inner, spiritual dimension. A person who wishes to study Kabbalah should already have an inner understanding of the ideas, and he must pursue the study of Kabbalah in a spirit of purity and holiness, in order to become a suitable vessel.

Glossary to *Learning from The Tanya: Volume Two in the Definitive Commentary on the Moral and Mystical Teachings of a Classic Work of Kabbalah*

The Kabbalah is full of stories about the birth of souls, with keen insights into the period of the fetus and of suckling, the need for a proper weaning and eventual growth into independence of thought and will. There is a first growth and a second growth, with definite stages. Most of the stages of growth of the physical organs are accomplished in concealment (before the development of consciousness), while the stages of growth of the soul, in its larger scope, are accomplished as adults. That is, the soul in the adult must go through its own stages of embryonic growth and suckling, then by the mental development, first of the smaller mind and then of the larger mind. There are kabbalistic works that see this growth in specific stages as a cosmic principle. They give detailed accounts of the growth of the year, its cycles and seasons, days move through embryonic periods, suckling, and stage after stage of development.

"The Power to Accept," in *In the Beginning: Discourses on Chasidic Thought*

Jewish mysticism never really became a separate domain of spiritual life outside the religious tradition. This may be due to the fact that the initial revelation at Mount Sinai was holy in such a way that it could never be shaken off. The Torah scriptures, at all levels of their composition, from the Bible to the Talmud and the latest commentaries of the sages, succeeded in retaining and elaborating this experience so profoundly that there was not much room for an emotional mysticism, either private or cultic, to develop on its own, outside of the established religious form.

"Mysticism in the Jewish Tradition," in *On Being Free*

The Scriptures, beginning with the Bible and including the many works of exegesis and commentary — such as the Talmud, the Kabbalah, and other writings — occupy such a central and special place in Judaism that the Hebrew name for this sacred literature, Torah, cannot be adequately translated into any other language. As someone once aptly summed it up: Other religions have a concept of scripture as deriving from Heaven, but only Judaism seems to be based on the idea that the Torah Scripture is itself Heaven. In other words, the Torah of the Jews is the essence of Divine revelation; it is not only a basis for social, political, and religious life, but is in itself something of supreme value.

"Torah," in *The Thirteen Petalled Rose: A Discourse on the Essence of Jewish Existence and Belief*

All the parts of the Torah are essential. They are not just complementary or supportive of each other; they also use different means, different languages, to say the same thing, whether it is Halakhah or Kabbalah, Mishnah or Zohar. For example, the prayer book has this formula for performing a *mitzvah*: "To unite the Holy One, blessed be He, and the Shekhinah." This is a kabbalistic formula. And it signifies that this union of Divine manifestation is the same single purpose of all our actions, no matter which of the *mitzvot* are involved. The scope of the Torah is always beyond any of its parts. It is always the same and it is possible to approach it, to view it, from many different angles.

"Mysticism in the Jewish Tradition," in *On Being Free*

Elijah's introduction to Tikunei Zohar uses the metaphor of the human body for the *sefirot*. Other chapters of the Tikunei Zohar employ other symbols and terms as well. But those used by Elijah are the most common — in both the Zohar and other works of Kabbalah — for they present the complete matrix of the "image of God."

"Patach Eliyahu — Elijah Began," in *The Thirteen Petalled Rose: A Discourse on the Essence of Jewish Existence and Belief*

The manifestations of the soul are, as we have seen, separate from the essence, but this does not imply that they are simply vehicles by means of which it is revealed. There is a wide range of fundamentally different manifestations of the soul, including intellect, feelings, cognitive powers, speech, and action. In order to understand their nature, one must clarify what is involved in the process of revealing.

The image used in earlier kabbalistic and chasidic works to describe revealing is that of *garbing*. The distinction between the two concepts, *garbing* and *revealing*, is extremely important. The implication of *revealing* in the sense in which it is normally used is that the entity itself, in its essence, is made apparent, is uncovered, and that there is no intermediary between it and the perceiver. *Garbing*, on the other hand, refers to a situation in which there is precisely such an intermediary, a *garment*. The garment is a separate entity, although it generally possesses no character or personality of its own: It serves as an instrument, whose function is to reveal the nature and the goal of another entity.

"The Psychology of the Soul," in *The Strife of the Spirit*

Sexual relations have an enormous influence on the soul. Not all human activities have an intrinsic inner connection. There are all kinds of activities that are rather insignificant; one example would be taking a walk. But sex is not one of those activities. Sex has an impact which is not only subjective; it is also something objective. Sex is a meaningful deed. In kabbalistic literature, descriptions of any deep connection between spiritual entities use the term *copulation*. The sexual relation in itself is an expression of a basic drive which, in Kabbalah, is called the *sefirah* of *yesod*. It is the power, the compelling desire, which comes from making connections. In that sense, sex is considered the supreme format for all forms of connection. It is one of those things that make a complete world.

"Sex is a Meaningful Deed," in *Parabola: The Search for Meaning*, Vol. 32:2

Among the first words of the Bible (Genesis 1:2) we have: "And the earth was without form and void." The Hebrew expression *tohu* (without form) has a more extensive meaning in the writings of the Kabbalah, where it denotes the world of chaos or original substance and energy that preceded Genesis. It was only with the collapse of this world of *tohu* that our world, the world of *tikun* (restitution), could come into existence. But the confrontation between the primal disorder and the amended order continues as a fundamental feature of reality.

Introduction to *In the Beginning: Discourses on Chasidic Thought*

In some *midrash* exegesis it is said that Adam at first reached from one end of the world to the other, but that after sinning, God put His hand on him and Adam's size was diminished to the human stature. The Kabbalah deals with the matter as a principle concerning the nature of man. A man should strive to penetrate beyond the fourth dimension of time into the fifth dimension of experience, where he reaches the other extreme of existence — original being. Instead, the range of human experience — the stature of man — extends only so far as his ego reaches.

"The Great Awe of Pachad Yitzchak," in *In the Beginning: Discourses on Chasidic Thought*

The fundamental dynamics of life and existence, according to the Kabbalah, is not a simple straight line process, either horizontal or from above to below. There is a complex interrelationship of actions and reactions, multiple influences and contextual forces that operate on a number of dimensions and levels. Essentially it is a mutuality of influence, hardly ever a one-way cause and effect and, as said, it is not confined to the human, or even the biological spheres; it is a cosmic way. There is no rising of the feminine waters of Isaac (Malchut, or Earth) except they be "drawn" by the upper waters of Abraham. And vice versa. The thinking here points to a conception that overturns the thermodynamic law of entropy, claiming as it does that there isn't just a one-way inevitable cooling influence of the active on the passive, but that the passive, in reacting, creates new situations. Abraham did not give birth to Isaac, he enabled him to be born; he acted on the feminine passive and thereby provided the possibility for Isaac to come into the world. Isaac's soul took advantage of the opportunity and came into the world to express that which was Isaac.

"The Power to Accept," in *In the Beginning: Discourses on Chasidic Thought*

Customarily, we speak of the different ways of dealing with Torah, from the explicit to the implicit, from *peshat* (literal meaning) to *derash* (exegesis), to *remez* (hint), to *sod* (secret or esoteric truth). All these simply address the same words of Scripture in four different languages, all of which have the same meaning. One of the methods of study is to gain an understanding of the way these languages change from one form of expression to another, how they change from saying something in poetic terms to those of a story, a commandment, and a kabbalistic idea. Consequently, the common view about mysticism and Kabbalah being a different world from the Talmud is a misconception of the organic unity of the whole. The Kabbalah and the Talmud are different forms of expression, each following its own point of departure.

"Mysticism in the Jewish Tradition," in *On Being Free*

When I discuss matters that are tangible and open for all to see and appreciate, things that are already "revealed," it is simple for others to verify the truth of what I say. But if I am talking about angels, for example, I must be very careful. If I speculate from ignorance, what I say will be nonsense. And it may become dangerous nonsense if I fail to realize the power and meaning of what I am saying and end up defiling the Majesty of God. Equally as esoteric as its subject matter is the language of Kabbalah. It is presented as a stream of abstract formulas, conveyed in Kabbalah's own unique jargon, understood only by a select cadre of scholars trained to decipher it. To avoid misunderstanding, Kabbalah had to be taught one on one by a master teacher singularly attuned to the capabilities and receptivity of each student. One cannot simply open the classic kabbalistic texts and glean their truths in a vacuum. Unfortunately, today Kabbalah has been commercialized by those who pretend to grasp its innermost secrets. These pretenders purport to teach — and to sell — what they do not understand, to people who are not equipped to receive it.

An essay, "Kabbalah for Today?"

There are relatively few places where Kabbalah can be studied properly, and the secondary literature available on the subject tends to be superficial, un-Jewish, or even anti-Jewish. While recent rabbinic authorities have ruled that study of "the doctrine of hidden things" need not be suppressed, it is nonetheless advisable to avoid getting into mysticism in an unbalanced way. One drawn to Judaism along the mystical path should take special pains to study Halakhah as well, particularly the Talmud and its commentaries, both in order to better understand the Kabbalah itself — a connection a number of well-known scholars have underscored — and in order to keep one's balance and avoid going astray. It is false and misleading to view the Jewish mystical tradition apart from the larger context of Judaism as a whole.

"Talmud Torah," in *Teshuvah: A Guide for the Newly Observant Jew*

Today, most of us are simply incapable of comprehending Kabbalah. The question is: Is there some way we, too, can 'receive' the remarkable teachings of Kabbalah in a meaningful way, without treading upon its Divine essence? One answer lies in the chasidic approach. It is a basic kabbalistic concept that the human soul is, in a manner, a spark of Divine revelation within the world and that each human being is a microcosm of the entire universe. Chasidism shows how the rarified teachings of Kabbalah, which speak to the macro-universe, can be adapted into a structure with ethical and practical meaning for our lives. In this way, Chasidism is a form of applied Kabbalah. Just as the Revealed Law frames the behavior of our bodies, the internalization of kabbalistic notions of the Hidden Law can attune us to our soul, educating it to connect with the Divine. In this model, the power of Kabbalah is harnessed not to serve our own desires but to align them with the wishes of the Almighty. One of the most important chasidic books is Zohar Chai (The Living Zohar). That is what Chasidism does: It gives the Kabbalah life by translating it into something meaningful in one's relationships with others and, most important, something that can quell the strife within one's own soul and calm the struggle of one's inner being.

An essay, "Kabbalah for Today?"

The truth is that the Kabbalah permeates every aspect of Judaism, and the esoteric wisdom has been a basic ingredient of scripture, ritual, and prayer. Even many popular expressions, in Hebrew but also in the colloquial Yiddish, have their source in the Kabbalah.

"Mysticism in the Jewish Tradition," in *On Being Free*

Mystery or mystical experience may simply be the way one sees certain truths. For some people the most revealed of Torah passages is full of secret meaning and wrapped in unfathomable mystery; for others, even the most esoteric wisdom is bright and clear, with nothing mysterious about it. The Baal Shem Tov used to say: The numerical value of *sod* (secret) is exactly that of *ohr* (light).

"Mysticism in the Jewish Tradition," in *On Being Free*

Books in English by Rabbi Adin Even-Israel Steinsaltz

Biblical Images: Men & Women of the Book
The Candle of God: Discourses on Hasidic Thought
Change & Renewal: The Essence of the Jewish Holidays,
    Festivals & Days of Remembrance
A Dear Son to Me: A Collection of Speeches and Articles
The Essential Talmud
A Guide to Jewish Prayer
In the Beginning: Discourses on Chasidic Thought
Learning from the Tanya: Volume Two in the Definitive
    Commentary on the Moral and Mystical Teachings of a
    Classic Work of Kabbalah
The Long Shorter Way: Discourses on Chasidic Thought
The Miracle of the Seventh Day
My Rebbe
On Being Free
Opening the Tanya: Discovering the Moral and Mystical Teachings
    of a Classic Work of Kabbalah
The Passover Haggada
Reference Guide to the Talmud
The Seven Lights: On the Major Jewish Festivals
Simple Words: Thinking About What Really Matters in Life
The Strife of the Spirit
The Sustaining Utterance: Discourses on Chasidic Thought
The Tales of Rabbi Nachman of Bratslav
Talks on the Parasha

KABBALAH

Talmudic Images
Teshuvah: A Guide for the Newly Observant Jew
The Thirteen Petalled Rose: A Discourse on the Essence of
    Jewish Existence and Belief
Understanding the Tanya
We Jews: Who Are We and What Should We Do

The Woman of Valor: Eshet Hayil

Rabbi Adin Even-Israel Steinsaltz is best known for his translation of and commentary on the Tanakh, the Babylonian Talmud, and the Mishneh Torah.

Arthur Kurzweil is author of *On the Road with Rabbi Steinsaltz* and *Pebbles of Wisdom from Rabbi Adin Steinsaltz*. He has also written *The Torah for Dummies*, *Kabbalah for Dummies*, and *From Generation to Generation: How to Trace Your Jewish Genealogy*.

www.ingramcontent.com/pod-product-compliance
Lightning Source LLC
Chambersburg PA
CBHW060431050426
42449CB00009B/2248